Signposts & Hedges

poems by

David Melville

Finishing Line Press
Georgetown, Kentucky

Signposts & Hedges

For Katie and Finn

Copyright © 2025 by David Melville
ISBN 979-8-89990-124-9 First Edition
All rights reserved under International and Pan-American Copyright Conventions. No part of this book may be reproduced in any manner whatsoever without written permission from the publisher, except in the case of brief quotations embodied in critical articles and reviews.

Publisher: Leah Huete de Maines
Editor: Christen Kincaid
Cover Art: Frank Tauran
Author Photo: Katie Melville
Cover Design: Elizabeth Maines McCleavy

Order online: www.finishinglinepress.com
also available on amazon.com

Author inquiries and mail orders:
Finishing Line Press
PO Box 1626
Georgetown, Kentucky 40324
USA

Contents

Part One
The Break Up 1
Tohubohu 2
On A Deschutes County Road In Winter 4
How To Remember Your Life Preserver 5
Shelter 7
Summer In Gorge Country 8
Evening Near Denali 10
Twilight 11
Nabash 12
The Hemlock On Top of Cape Meares 13
On Zen Retreat 14
Silent Music 15

Part Two
Noon At Siuslaw Pond 19
Tasting At Cadenhead's Whisky Shop, Established 1842 20
What It's About 21
Blooms 24
Mexican Carnival 25
Compassion 28
The Crack 29
Yojo 30
Gulf 32

Part Three
Nirvana 35
Memento Mori 36
Sayulita Frigate 37
Precession 38
My Inferno 39
Purgatory 40
Steps 41

Part Four
Solace 45
Loppers 46
The Ones Who Walk 47
Visiting My Brother's Nebraska Farmstead 48
Lettuce 49
Bananas 50

Neruda On The Playa 51
Klamath Forest 53
Wedding March 54
Signposts And Hedges 55
45 56

Notes 58

Acknowledgments 62

About The Author 63

PART ONE

The Break Up

Those who like to get dirty,
roll with them.
Avoid the indifferent
whose breath seeps
in cold streams from the mouth.

Your earth's work is richer
than what is visible.
Toss a clod of turf
in the air. Watch
as the loam splits up,
falls to pieces . . .

Break yourself like that
in going against gravity:

if we don't, death
will break us anyway
when it's too late to fall into
what we could have become.

Tohubohu

When God clucked vowels from his belly
yowling his chutzpah and sprang
the universe open with his hullabaloo,
dawn cracked; earth was still molten,
ripe, ore smelted, thudding
igneous onto ice crusts, sullen places
where ash rained on rock
meant one day to nourish meadows:
foxglove, buttercups, hollyhocks.

It was then that something dark flitted,
a blur in the eye corner.

When God jumped,
it leapt, when he crouched,
it squatted, when he ducked,
it tucked chin and dove.
When he spoke,
it was a lip mimic, yucking
the first utterance, mouthing
secret syllables, and every hollow
rang with its undercurrent.
It was a hazy wiggle,
murky, malleable.
Lucifer—God named it,
light bringer.

And when God flung his seed,
the darkness slithered
into Eve's belly, and rolled
out with the womb splat,
then crawled pudgy-armed,
a ripple across veld grass.

Each yammer, it toothed
her sore nipple; when she slept,
it dozed, then crept on tip-toe
with Adam's footpads until she woke
and the trembling
followed behind them.

When they turned, it veered,
when they laughed, it cackled,
when they fucked, it thrust,
when they lazed, it sighed,
when they stole, it lied,
and they were happy
never quite to see it.

On A Deschutes County Road In Winter

Crossing that open country where mountains row up
like chorus girls, they each stood large on my road

this one sheer, the next cragged, the next slim bottomed, another
broad faced, another red topped, an elegant plump. With each

curve I traversed, skirting the troublesome faces and giving
wide berth to knife edges, admiring wild legs and canyons,

the wind shifted. Cloud boas dangled from fir shoulders,
then fluttered off, feather white. And I was twelve again,

stiff with the prospect of the slow dance and the cold sweat:
palms at basement parties cupped around a bony waist.

Revelation happens like that, in burlesque moments,
a grope for contact we want but are afraid to touch.

Then I knew it like my Ford pickup's ripped upholstery,
how, as night dropped its black negligee, somewhere

in the distance another would queue up, waiting to dance.

How to Remember Your Life Preserver

Those things you do
do them from the flow
of hidden waters that move
within you. All that you do
do from that river of joy.
Act from another spot,
and the blessing …
disappears. After all,
when you flail after others
you may swim towards the sunken
or worse, the drowning.
Reach for the rope

that love dangles—

Set aside your false will;
the willful sit in jail,
crabs in mesh traps
or fish who sizzle
in the skillet. And the cops
who haul them off in cuffs
sizzle with anger too,
alongside the simmering judge
who makes an example of the defiant
so that you will knuckle under
his grimace. Look past
displays like those
to the buoyant.
When self-will is released,
at last you may know
how you torture yourself.

Born at the well's bottom,
life begins in black waters.
Down under those stacked stones
how could you know
sunlight in an open field?

So insist no more on going
only where you want to go.
Ask your way to the river
where many currents
flow together in harmony.
There is a coast that opens
after it, reached only by floating

past snags and lulls,
shoals and tidepools,

out to that vast horizon
where you are infinite
yet borne in a single drop.

Shelter

Brown pools, warm, wide, those eyes
are what I remember most.
Sometime near dawn she must have stumbled
as she trotted through that tussock,
one foot caught in the coyote trap—
the cable's thin band, sheer and lethal
as garter lace. Beside the fence post
alongside the belt of wind-breaking cedars,
which wound through the barren hills,
Charlie knelt, sighing as he tried to unsnare
her hind hoof. Each pull, the slender wire
sank; each tug she made, that galvanized loop
pinched deeper. Then a blur of silver:

the stake popped loose, shot from dirt.
Impossibly as it whipped past
I caught it. My cousin caught my belt
and somehow, together, two boys held her,
our hands rubbed raw by wire.

To let go was to consign her
to the tangle of limb and needle,
hopelessly strung on pine boughs
in the shelter belt, the long wait for night,
eruption of yips: fang and claw.

We both stood our ground, the doe and us.
Buffalo grass swished against our coveralls.
Around our shins the pasture shifted, softly brushed
the creosote post. Blades, dun and long,
bent and waved in the prairie wind. Our breath
came in huffs.

The slow nod. He let go,
leveled the .22. My eyes never left those
wide pools until he lowered the barrel.
The wire sank—

a silver cord in winter grass.

Summer In Gorge Country

Land of burnt umbra,
striated rock, wind mutter,
snake-hot sun, grassless stone
under the sky's blue umbrella;

above, the falcon floats
on a bubble of nothingness—

wind pump, wing surge,
flap and glide.

Under those pinions
a river: the gift giver
whose blue hues froth oxygen,
liquid pockets of time
that drift where otter and beaver
flutter and flip-kick
past stone paths that lead
to the brown patches,

to eye grit and snake rattle,
the place where hills roll,
where fiery bubbles once
bulged from the volcanic bed,
suds red on the lava stream.

This land is a place
Heraclitus might like
where the sun wilts
the thousand native cadences
into grass whispers, hisses
at the edges of the swarthy mind

where we cannot step twice
on the same dust path,

where eroded sandstone
spirals into citadels of baked lime,
rifts and slots of canyon topos, plateaus
that submarine into granite boxes
where wind shear pierces
the arroyos and scrub pine,
habitat for coyote and field mice.

Yet on the horizon a plane floats
over the gorge country; its wing-tilt
blinks dobs of sunlight, an arrow shadow,
tapered shade that flickers over the dun hills
as though for all its elegant machinery
it could outrace time.

Evening Near Denali

Loon's song piques
my longing. I too flutter
so overcome with devotion
I want to haunt
the night with keening

but have nothing
so melodious to say.

Great mountain, I beg you,
sing me too.

Twilight

This precious moment—
happy on the porch
we sit, one soul

though seemingly two.

Between us life
flows like water:

garden's beauty,
bird song,
and overhead, stars …

Those white sparks
watch as we recollect
a time long forgotten
when our dust
was incandescent.

Without self,
unruffled by thoughts
we rest
until an empty belly
rumbles and we laugh.

One form we are
upon this earth,
another in a rich,
silent space.

Nabash

Do not blame Eve for the apple's poison bite:
the garden teemed with things God caused to be.
"Eat, my love, eat, and then we'll know what's right.

Why should it be that knowledge gives you fright?"
the serpent asked unwinding from the tree.
Blame Eve no more for the apple's poison bite.

"Have you wondered what lies beyond the night?
It's just a piece of fruit—no blasphemy.
Eat, my love, eat, to know what's wrong from right,"

his forked tongue whispered in the fading light.
Naïve and young, she listened, true, but please
do not blame Eve for the apple's poison bite.

Slowly, the serpent twined her shapely thighs:
"God's breath brushed me too. Would I deceive?
Eat, my love, eat, and then you'll know what's right.

The Truth has little taste without insight:
Or is there something you don't want to see?"
Do not blame Eve for the apple's poison bite.
Eat, my love, eat, and then we'll know what's right.

The Hemlock On Top Of Cape Meares

Knotted like nerves, roots hang
over the headland,

fibers that idly drift
over the Pacific's incessant roll

sloshing as winds, casual as Pollock,
splotch rocks with rain.

Stems which once sucked decay from dirt,
burls which once sipped so richly up these

wooden straws, now hollow with inner emptiness,
are not burdened that one

tomorrow or another they will slip
sudden from this grass perch

while claps applaud their teetering
from grey clouds on high

who bang loudly at their ineffable drop
as though to boom:

"This too is just so."

On Zen Retreat

Fur clings, clumped old carpet.
Specks flit, whir, stir again
on shoulder bone. Green stalks
poke cud. She munches,
swish-tailed, fly shooing—

Behind us on the hill
the cement block monastery
squats. I know from silence

the buddha is not just there:

He's nudging cud,
haunch-moist in pasture,
making milk from meadow grass.

The Silent Music

> *—in response to Ezra Pounds' war poem "Sestina: Altaforte"*

I.

To sit once more silent, legs crossed, at peace,
relaxed on the cushion, content as summer's music,
far from the juddering city, its unending clash
of horns (cars, trucks) honking, voices opposing,
shouts of drivers quarreling, their faces crimson.
Instead to sit, spine-straight, my heart rejoicing.

II.

Thoughts move across the mind: just watch them, rejoicing
at how like clouds they come and go. This peace
is here for all of us, even when thought's harsh music
becomes the roll of thunder, dark scud that flashes crimson,
and anger's lightning cracks like swords opposing.
Be the storm's watchful eye, the calm within the clash.

III.

Men are much in love, it seems, with the clash—
chests bumping, butt of horns, rejoicing
in strife, the race won, battle fought, two forces opposing.
Always striving for victory, they hope to obtain peace.
It's maya, my friends. Stop and face the music:
nothing beautiful's been built while drunk on blood's crimson.

IV.

So sip a different drink: the more potent crimson
wine of the Beloved. From that cup there is no clash,
no conflict when drunk on reading Rumi, just rejoicing,
whirling while the timbrel thrums to harmonium music.
And at the center of that spinning: peace,
though the arms may flare in directions opposing.

V.

When the sun reborn flares on the opposing
horizon, and field and wood turn crimson,
let us wake early and drink of that peace.
Birds throat their joy, even as their colored feathers clash
brightly against the flushed sky. Filled with rejoicing,
we'll plump our zafus and sit amidst their music.

VI.

Yet among larks and wrens I've found no music
like the hush that comes when the mind's through opposing
thought with thought. Calm descends. Rejoicing
begins as the hara bubbles and swells, then flares crimson.
In that sweet state, when reason and emotion no longer clash,
nothing exists—only the power of peace:

body and mind just empty, no more clash, no more opposing.
Only the heart's left rejoicing, a newborn in dawn's first crimson.
No, there is no music like the silent music of peace.

PART TWO

Noon At Siuslaw Pond

Half-asleep on the green bank, drowsing,
aware of nothing but that lilting laugh,

tilt of hip, lifted knee, the bunched dress,
and toes that stretch so elegant

in tree-shadowed light. Side by side,
as we laze in the warm woodland breeze,

wings appear in the hazed sun shafts—
orange grace; flutter and dive.

With each glide comes caution's hint:
how as it bobs and flits over pond water,

the stripes that tiger its saffron are held
toward heaven, each splotch to the sun.

When will I show my dark spots so boldly?
Go on. Your blots are also in love

with the joy of being exposed.

Tasting At Cadenhead's Whisky Shop, Established 1842

Peat smoke stokes earth fires in this American belly.
The iron-bound barrel taps a stream rush from Islay:
cascade of blade grass and bog water froths across rocks

straight into the dram glass. Nose the aqua vitae:
gold water, cask strength. Nostrils tickle with each bubble-glass'
pass, a nose so potent that the dram shop's floor boards

moan the sauced moans of ancestral ghosts. Each slow sip elicits
tongue licks from the tartan-clad, men like an ancient uncle
who limped, let's guess, from syphilis

caught from a frocked smock in some Edinburgh brothel.
Or perhaps he got his tilt-walk from the dirk shaft stuck in his calf
fifing for Bonnie Prince Charlie. Then again it might have been

covenanting for Cromwell, another roundhead pew-filling
at pistol point. Don't ask me; like my malt-lifting forefathers,
I'm half-soused.

What It's About

Walrus-waisted, the waitress
led us to our places,
white plastic placemats
splattered with gravy,
butter crusts, other gray matter.
She wiped twice and left.
Mary Beth sat on my lap,
eighteen, flat-chested
as a Rand McNally map.
We ordered cokes, fiddled straws.
I was drinking
green eyes when she shifted
to the other side of the booth:
"The hokey pokey. It scares me."

"Babe, next time I'll heat the truck."
"But it scares me."
"Someday when you've a ring
we'll do it in a real bed."
"Yes," she said, "but it frightens."

"My feelings," I said, "you know
they're hot as a barn fire,
fiery like I fessed when we was
parked by the bridge,
so hot that crick water
won't put them out."

"What if," she said, "what if,
that's what it's all about?"

"Put it in," I hummed:
"Shake it all about."
"Ain't you listening?"
"You know I is."

"Rolling on your seat, fooling
in that truck,
knocked up, plop a few out,
what if that's it? There ain't
nothing else?"

The waitress waddled
back with burgers—
hair like drier lint,
apron hanging.
Mary Beth watched her saunter off,
forehead crinkling
like our fries. "What if
I, me, someday look
like that? Waitressing here,
kid-raising. Dwaine,
that ain't no kind of life."

Glint of moss-green eyes.
My heart went tumbling out,
made off, tumbling
like crick water, flipping
over stones, whipping
under creosote, bubbling
past bridge planks, splashing off.
My heart gurgled on those
moss stones.

"So much hay rolling's
coming your way, Mary Beth.
Me, some other fella,
fellas of all kinds,
big, short, skinny, fat,
lined up here to Dallas. So much
loving's heading your way
you won't care one fig
when you get pear-hipped,
milky eyed. Might be
why sagging happens.

Bodies start out tight.
Lovin's what loosens them up.
Droops are drops of life."

She soaked a fry
dabbed it up red,
liquidy as my heart.
"Me," I says, "I ain't got nothing
on the hokey pokey."

She hopped back on my lap,
poked a fry between my lip,
fingered my string tie.

She hummed, bubbling
like crick water.

"Loving," she smiled,
"that's what it's all about."

Blooms

Laugh
with more
than lips.

Laugh
whole-bodied
like the rose.

Laugh
from each hip
and petal.

Laugh
root, stem,
and thorn.

Laugh
perennially through
winter

with
beauty pruned
and gone.

Laugh
with your whole self
until

no self
is there to laugh
at all.

Mexican Carnival

Henpecked and paddy whacked, I sit
boot shod on the Octopus,
a tentacled ferris wheel that spins

notions from noggins, whirling—

bumblefooted hit of a bongwater dream.
Children scream. The car tips.
We flip. Grease drips

down the egg-shaped sides

of this inverted submarine. Dangling
restrained by the rusted bar,
suddenly she is mine again—

fingers curled in my palm
like the January nights
she'd slipped against my chest

and we were two

cupped Cs. Whipsawed upright
I brace. Spinning,
thrown flat against the cage,

I choke back vertigo's aftertaste

as grill slats press diamonds in my cheek
like the one I'd hoped would dot
her knuckle. The seat spins,

then tips.

Palms grip the cold bar,
frantic to quiet metallic rattle.
Strung lights leave

neon slurry, red bulbs

lace the Nayarit night.
Gravity rights. We pause
above hawker's cries, floating

over barker stalls filled with
popcorn and pink purses,
the bear I would have plucked
from the glass box

with long tongs to hand her.

Then to ping-pong again,
whipsawed by the thought,
She's gone

to slather a barber,

fuzz bump a shoe company exec,
someone who'll make her
dimple-wide happy. Slammed

by this trajectory I sense

the cage that contains me.
Beyond is calm. In that lull
I repose in mechanical arms,

afloat on the Octopus,

the dusk studded—
a thousand jeweled fingers.
I hover

over knife throwers,

fire eaters, goateed ladies
until we drift down
slowly to the dirt

and the carnie braces

my cage as it comes
shuddering to a stop.
The bar lifts. A one-toothed smile.

I am released into the carnival night.

Compassion

Our sun drops
fire seeds: succulent light
that reddens pavement,
reddens the folds of plants,
and yet we long

for deeper warmth,
snug as lovers' arms,
curve of elbow,
slender or strong,
lust's fit, tightly cupped.

Blankets cover me
each night as I slip
beneath fleece sheets,
and still I ask, Beloved,
for your return:

press your dove-heat
down, breath on bone.
Pluck me once more

from myself. Rip
back these veils of murk.
Lace your tender balm
across my chest.

Dear one, I want—
no—I need you.
Come now.
Hear my call.

The Crack

Those drowsy mornings, sun's
blaze in the eye,
hot tinder in the mind—
sleep's narcotic fog, a blot
burst through—

needle through gauze.

Still groggy from the stupor
of a thousand wanton nights,
I wonder:

when at last
will the curtain draw back?
When will I awake?

Yojo

>—Ode to Queequeg's idol, *Moby Dick, Chp. 10*

You sit there on the Nantucket table,
ebony idol, god plucked from the supposed
cannibal's topcoat pocket,
immaculate tiki, who first cut wave-white

in some New Zealand outrigger
to arrive in grim-skied New England,
borne afloat a Haitian frigate, lugged
upriver on junkets, Da Pek to Nan King,
having visited a thousand Pacific dots,
doted on in Fiji, Tasmania, Tahiti;
sands that you, Yojo, impossibly
hauled from the ocean's churning blue,
eons before sun-browned hands whittled you.

Those brows, thick-carved with tropic experience—
palms, typhoons, orange suns—
and the whorls that fierce your face,
etched with reverence, a world apart
from this American bonanza of
six packs, barbeques, bottled pills.

How I would trade closets of lapels,
kitchen ladles, claw-foot tubs,
cereal brands, designer labels, even all
the verified scientific instruments of earth—
telescopic sitings of Mars, magnified bacteria cells—
to know . . .

                god does inhabit the wood,
haunts the branch, still rests quietly
in buffalo grass, not just in ayahuasca
or peyote, but other leaves besides the toked
smoke of cannabis. At last I might hear
each oak ring with rain . . .

how each bole
holds you, Yojo, holy basin
for heavens' downpour, for the dews
that seep the log, resting spot for crows
who purple the bark with hemlock.
Saw a tree; see the sky.
How better life might be if
we all bowed low to a log;

for what is God's word?
Alpha and omega engraved on grain,
etched packets of pulp once Gutenberg broke
time's wall to make god's word
graven image on idle wood.
Wood holds the words that whirl the world.

Still, you run wilder than any tongue
or groove. Nestled in vein and burl,
you go where you would
hidden beneath lacquer, tucked under varnish,
unseen potence of pulpit and crib,
nailed as the cross, or minbar of mosque,
and at last sanded down fine
for the coffin, that last whale-ship
which cradles us, a raft

of polished pine which hauls us
rolling, sliding, drifting up swells
until we tip over the rift,
waterlogged into the bottomless.

Gulf

When I spoke of the heart, that raucous ocean that froths,
heedless and repetitious as a drunk,
open mouthed, pounding foam by the barrel, gathering
to roar sloshed, mad-libbed secrets,
more sound than sense, until the curl, the slump,
the bubbled sigh . . .
and when I babbled about palapas,
islanders who rise with the sun to sweep the sands of fronds,

I'd meant you as that turbulent water,
me the palm-heaper, an island resident.
But metaphors walk backwards.
There you are, walking, sun
browning your spine, fingers touching
coconut husks, arms crooked, filled with fronds.

PART THREE

Nirvana

Better than chewing bull pizzle
or licking salt from a sow's ear,
husk of skin, ink stamp
tattooing the blue feedlot number
on the pig's ridged lobe—
a treat to polish the choppers,
unfreshen the breath,
chip the tartar.

I was better than that:

better even than gnawed frisbee,
mawed tennis balls,
stuffed lion,
the bristle-furred hedgehog,
loved so much.
Better
even than the tether
that bound us,
hand and collar.

Dogs don't need to die
to find their heaven.
It was here—
on the house porch,
the park grass,
the naugahyde couch—
wherever
we were together.

Memento Mori

Recall the thin grey worm will be here soon
slip-sliding right across my breathless nose
and everything I love will be in ruin.

This life I spend asleep, so unattuned
to nature and myself; and yet I doze.
Recall the thin grey worm will be here soon.

Like a cold, starless night without a moon,
the mind blanks when I contemplate all those
precious loves that will one day be in ruin:

books, friends, oak forests . . . you. My heart's cocoon,
unpierced by loss, is lost from love. And so
recall once more: the worm will be here soon.

Last night, our quarrel: I became the loon,
petty, lost. I forgot what wise men know:
one day hence all I love will be in ruin.

It's not too late, though life may be past noon—
I'm here, and you. The light in us can grow.
Recall the thin grey worm will be here soon
and everything I love will be in ruin.

Sayulita Frigate

Aloft, dark wings, a jagged shadow
that hovers over the offal:
intestines, innards, paper-thin organ tissue,

and the bright pink heart
of freshly gutted dorado.
Diving steeply, she lands

with a swoop that scatters
the clustering grey gulls.
Among their squawks, awkward flaps,

the sharp quill of her beak starts to scratch
gill and guts, then casually she hops off
with the carcass. How many dawns

did it take for the silver-haired
Mexican fisherman who sliced this fish
to learn not to flinch after he first

jumped his dinghy's gunwale,
wading to shore through low,
churning breakers as even then,

she arrived, her fine point
brought to bear like some Mayan scribe,
but to calmly haul his gutted catch

along the sand's unfurling scroll
while behind him she began
to etch in that stark script?

Precession

When the strong-haunched lion lies down
      with the lamb,
when repentant Cain pulls Abel close
      in a warm bear hug;
    when brother loves brother;
          sister no longer gets gobbled;
          and the wolf
    laps no more with its haggard tongue;
          the maggot no longer
            jiggles its pale, slow way into stagnant vein,
          dead sinew;
    larvae no longer wriggle and drop
        eggs in animal skins;
          bacteria no longer swim in fetid pools; round filarial worms
        no longer poke heads from African shins,
        and men
        no longer poke unasked in wombs;
        liars' lips are kept jaw-tight;
    when the Palestinian weds the Jew;
      and the Christian actually
        listens to Christ
      chin dipped in unselfish prayer,
the pole star may have already
      slipped south.
    All-suffering earth may have shed its wanton,
        bloody children by then.
        Its orbit may no longer wobble
              or totter.
        Perfect peace at last
        on this world will
          descend.

My Inferno

Woe's gates are aptly marked: put aside
hope all who enter here. I walk alone
in monochrome dusk—no love or guide—

to cross death's stream and join those spirits blown
off course by lust's illicit touch, then go
farther down towards dark sins I disown.

Here's some I've known: the one who grumbles so
in Styx's thick mud; the heretic who burns
inside a flaming tomb; the man who chokes

on Sodom's ashen rain. Now fraud's winged worm
waits to gyre me lower down. "Debauched!"
my deeper demons each call out in turn:

"Watch how he chews himself with guilt and doubt;
both Judas and the tooth of Satan's mouth."

Purgatory

> "Ma Virgilio n'avea lasciati sceemi—
> But Virgil had left us, he was no longer there—"
>
> —from Canto XXX, in which the pagan Virgil must return
> to the underworld having led Dante to heaven

Wince not for Virgil solemn on his march
from heaven, the ramble and stumble down slope,
last rays on his neck, and judgment's gap a stark

crack in the earth; inferno without hope.
Behind him, pilgrim Dante soars to joy
in folds of pure light: angelic throats

whose music rings in blissful, holy voice,
with all existence one vast dream in song.
Yet Dante shall slip down again, psalm destroyed,

bereft of Beatrice, his dead love gone.
At last each poet comes to know the fruits
of paradise are rarely tasted long:

Though saints and lovers sing devoted truths,
artists' souls ever sink back to earth.

Steps

Those days I snuck a glimpse of paradise,
crept slowly, step by step, up the creaky stair
and having reached the door, with squinting eye,

knelt beneath the round keyhole to stare
in child-like wonder at that dazzling sight
which soothed my heart, for once I was aware,

no longer climbing blindly up the flight,
but conscious of the love my ego mars.
What there I saw besides that pure light,

translucent as a distant fiery star,
resides beyond my power to convey,
and yet—though it was lightning in a jar—

when I recall the blessing of those days,
I am that flash, the heavenly display.

PART FOUR

Solace

Last night I dreamed
I made love to the trees,
akimbo in the rustle,
must of leaf, skin of bark,

as overhead, sister moon
rose early
to offer a peek
to brother sun

whose fingers had just reached
the round glow of her face

and slipped off.

What woke me I could not say:
night bump, creep of animal,
branches with their slow scrapes
against pane…

One bright day we too will
rise and shine
in love with our orbit,
delighting in each moment
of touch, confident
in our starry course.

Loppers

Loppers clop and clip
thick green branches caught on top
gutters that cup rain.

The Ones Who Walk

>   —in Memorium Ursula K. Le Guin

They walked away from Omelas,
red roofed with fruit-hung trees—
yes, left a golden paradise
never to be seen,

forsook that bright-towered city,
thinking they were being kind.
They sped so far from Omelas
to leave its glitch behind.

They chose to go from Omelas—
gulped down that bitter pill.
To walk, they thought, was medicine,
though the child lived there still.

Miles unknown from Omelas
still haunted by bleak cries,
the filthy hole in Omelas,
the child left inside,

they knew the price of happiness
was what the hole concealed;
round they turned for Omelas,
facing what was real.

Back they walked to Omelas—
sniffles, wretched cries—
to feel the hurts the child felt,
and heal the heart's divide.

**Visiting My Brother's Nebraska Farmstead
On August 30th At Dusk**

Stars drop
like salt
on tablecloth.
The hay
is pitched,
bucked in bales
I can barely make out
in the green field
where the cricket
flicks its thighs
at the lone
porch light.

The hoarse toad
bloats
from the moss pond.

At once, I know
I am of the earth tonight.

Lettuce

Doctors will tell you
to eat your lettuce.

Deep leafy greens heal
all that ails. Try lettuce

spread with garlic,
balsamic or oil. Let us

eat heaps of broccoli too to make up
for the booze, the pills that led us

to this place—life's middle swath—
where sprigs of lettuce

must satisfy us. Iced sweets
build paunch but lettuce

wards all, cures all,
soothes all. So don't let up:

cud the leaves bovine-like
as long as life lets us.

Bananas

Jungle vine twines like lovers' legs
around a trunk bunched with clumped bananas.

The skin of curved fruit stays green in this sultry heat
until plucked by primates hungry for ripe bananas

like the monkey who clutches two per fist and hangs
by a tail between palm fronds. Some say he is bananas.

Psychologists conducted a study among college students
handing out boxes of donuts and a tub of gold bananas.

The men, naturally, fed on donuts, their faces slicked
with glazed holes. The women, of course, preferred bananas.

Even at dinner we are driven by latent desire;
the proof, they say, is in a long curved banana

except that young women diet and watch their figures. I, like Freud,
figure that a cigar is sometimes a cigar, a banana a banana.

Neruda On The Playa

This was the day I took Pablo to the beach,
the rush of sea a short walk
past the hacienda garden where in ficus
sat the iguana,
where green scales
glowed in Sayulita sun,
the tongue tasting aery nada
under frigate wings, those dark birds
which boomeranged over the ficus.

In my lap—dirtied by pebbles,
tacos, cocoa lotion—
Pablo sat. Pages flapped. I paid him
no attention. He was patient.
Pablo knew a thing or two about distractions,
how a glimpse of nothing
beneath wet cloth
intoxicates more than the merely naked.

Such is the power of revelation.
Bikinis wait for lovers:
the reptile touch, the air-licking tongue,
the spokes radiating from spine
like a crowned sun,
the delicate scale shimmer,
the whip tail,
warmth basking,
the dewlap upside down
from its chin.

Had Pablo wrote an iguana ode
(he might have, I don't know),
he would have praised that green nose,
the salt gland, the night vision.
He would saved most exuberant praise
for the forehead:
the third eye
unblinking
as it saw me as a boy

when I took a stone, palmed it
at a robin who lifted calmly,
then flapped back on the fence post
as the rock smashed the farmhouse window.
Pablo would have praised
the unblinking eye
that knows where my stones will go.

We lavish praise
most on that we lack.
We praise with a tongue
that hints of the none.
The nada under wings.
The none under stones.
The none under nostrils
that sniff
aery nothing.
The none under sea rush,
under tree bark.
The none beneath
bikini linings.
The none in the eye that
blinks
as it spots there the cosmos,
whose intoxicating secrets
lovers are shown.
The none that births all,
births
tree, beach, sea.
That darts in ficus.
The none from whence.
The everything.
The nada.

Klamath Forest

Trunk to trunk, woods roll past
alert soldiers in
leaf-plumed helmets
perked to the beat
of a radiant drummer.
Rooted, they suck
smoke-stack disorder.
Peace-wagers rise above us.

Wedding March

Love is to rend
a hundred veils,
draw back the gossamer
which sunders—
the sheer nothing
which separates—
you from I.

And when your face appears
luminous
in its hue of flowers—
invitation of the new bride—

the one
for whom I've sought
all those turnings of the clock,
whose kiss is grace
and calls me home
after what seems
a thousand lives,

then when the overture
fades to silence—
rumble of snares,
thrum of lyres
dies—

I will tumble into
loving arms which
seem as though
they were always
already mine.

Signposts And Hedges

The wealth of being here: plump cherries that droop
fat-bellied from leaves, green spears whose tips stretch
dream-ward for one dance with the dangling moon,
ochre roses over concrete walks

that run north by northwest to the old town square
where quart milk cartons catch on park bench legs
beneath lonely men with little cash to spare,
and further on to barns with rooster cages,

rust-red barrels, snarls, yips on gravel roads,
past stiff-stalked fields and slow, one-lane traffic
to hills that rise above the last signpost.
Don't say I should turn back on this flesh magic—

leave this body's toils, loves, grievous hurts—
for an Eden unlike this wild, delicious earth.

45

When that old record
whirls its grooves,
whines again,
patterns spin,
and the steel pin
sets off grunts,
sobs of snot, and howls
out blues forlorn
as any Billie groan—
tracks worn dim from spiraling
again, again, again—
only then may you
jolt up

needle skip

find it's not just you,
scratched, alone
in your isolation booth;

it's our roots, this soil
we share, rocks rubbed flat
by moon currents
tugged hither and yon
by our mother's spin,

and those stars
arms stretched

wide like a girl's milky skin
as she whirls on the summer lawn,

our whole galactic mass
spinning,

ancient dervish
whirling
around a hole
where all
is perfectly
still.

Notes

Most of these poems are free verse, meaning, they do not adhere to the traditional conventions of meter and form; but some of them do. These notes offer a few tips about those written in form and provide a guide to the less obvious allusions.

"The Break Up" and "How To Remember Your Life Preserver" found their inspiration in some lines of Jalal al-Din Rumi, the great Sufi poet who lived in Persia between 1207 and 1273. A few others offer a wink or a nod toward Rumi.

"Tohubohu" is the word for the murky chaos that reigns at the beginning of Genesis 1:2. It is the anglicized form of the actual Hebrew, which is *tohu-wa-bhohu*.

"Summer In Gorge Country" makes reference to Heraclitus, the ancient Greek philosopher who lived in the fifth century B.C. in Ephesus (now modern-day Turkey). It was Heraclitus who observed one cannot step into the same river twice.

"Shelter" features a shelter belt. Farmers and ranchers on the American plains once planted pines, a few trunks deep, along pastures or fields, especially during the Great Depression, to block the fierce prairie winds. Longer and wider than a wind break, these stout bands of spruce or cedar came to be known as shelter belts.

"Nabash" is the ancient Hebrew word for "serpent." At several points in the Torah, it appears as the word for snake, while the actual word for Eve's tempter in Genesis 3:1 is the strikingly similar *nachash*, which means something like "the shining one." "Nabash" is a villanelle, a poetic form in which the beginning line and the third line alternate to become each of the next four stanzas' last lines. At a villanelle's close, the repeated lines return once more, now side by side, to end the poem.

'The Silent Music" is a sestina. This intricate form was invented by troubadours in the High Middle Ages. Each line's end word rotates in a fixed order in the next stanza until the cycle completes and all of the end words come back once more to compose the entire final stanza. "Sestina: Altaforte" by Ezra Pound, the most widely admired sestina in English, celebrates warfare by channeling the voice of Bertran de Born (c. 1140

- 1215), a real Medieval troubadour whom Dante Alighieri sent to his *Inferno's* eighth circle for fomenting division and strife. The sestina here uses Pound's same end words in the same order as Pound, but to invoke peace.

"My Inferno," "Purgatory," and "Steps" mirror the three stages of the *Divine Comedy* by Dante Alighieri, who wrote in Italy in the thirteenth century. For the *Divine Comedy*, Dante created an interlocking rhyme scheme called terza rima. The outside lines of each stanza rhyme with each other, while the middle line becomes the rhyme for the next stanza. Thus, the first stanza's pattern of a/b/a turns into b/c/b for the second stanza, followed by c/d/c for the third, and so on. These three poems are terza rima sonnets, a sonnet form created in 1820 by Percy Bysshe Shelley, who adapted Dante's rhyme scheme for his "Ode to the West Wind."

"My Inferno" winds its way down along the descending levels of hell in the *Divine Comedy*. At the bottom of Dante's hell, Satan, trapped in ice, eternally chews Judas in one of his fanged mouths.

"Purgatory" mentions two characters in the *Divine Comedy*, both real people. Virgil was the Roman poet who wrote *The Aeneid* during the reign of Caesar Augustus, several centuries before Dante turned him into his guide through the first two stages of the afterlife. At the top of Mount Purgatory, Dante discovers Virgil has disappeared, unable as a pagan to ascend into paradise. The role of guide is then assumed by a real woman, Beatrice Portinari, who was the love of Dante's life. She died of an illness in Florence at the age of 25, while Dante was still a young man. Now a saint, she takes over for Virgil and leads Dante on into the heavenly spheres.

"Tasting At Cadenhead's" makes reference to the real whisky shop founded by William Cadenhead in 1842. As Scotland's oldest independent bottler, Cadenhead's sells whisky from casks, more pure and potent than bottled whisky, and until quite recently, unavailable in America. Islay (pronounced "eye-la") is an island in the Hebrides, known for the smokiness of its single malts. Bonnie Prince Charlie was Charles Edward Stuart, a Scottish claimant to the English throne, who in 1746 spurred the last great Scottish uprising against the British at the Battle of Culloden. Oliver Cromwell, a Puritan, ruled Britain as Lord Protector from 1654 to 1658 during the brief overthrow of the monarchy after the English Civil War. Known for their their flat or close-cropped hair, his supporters were nicknamed roundheads.

"Mexican Carnival'" makes reference to Nayarit, which is a Mexican province along its Pacific coast.

"Yojo" is the carved wooden idol of Queequeg, the companion and bosom friend of Ishmael, the narrator of Herman Melville's *Moby Dick*. In search of a berth on a whaler, Ishmael meets Queequeg in a New England inn where they share a room and where Queequeg, a South Pacific islander, spends a day-long ritual in reverence of Yojo. From sun up to sun down, Queequeg, unmoving on his knees, contemplates Yojo. Near the novel's end, Yojo is featured again as Queequeg carves his own coffin. Gutenberg, referred to in this poem, is Johannes Gutenberg (1393 – 1468), who invented the moveable-type printing press, which he used to make beautifully bound Bibles.

"Gulf" is a free-verse sonnet. With 14 lines, a sonnet, traditionally written in iambic pentameter (though this one is not) is typified by a turn of mood around line eight.

"Memento Mori" is a Latin phrase for "remember you must die." In spiritual traditions, ranging from Plato to Tibetan to Christian Europe, it is also a contemplative practice for remembering the transitory nature of life. Like "Nabash," this poem is a villanelle.

"Precession" is the phenomenon where the earth's axis wobbles, ever so slowly, as it spins, much like a top. As a consequence, the earth's orientation among the stars shifts over the course of millennia so that our own north stars points towards true north only some of the time during this great cycle, which takes some 25,000 years.

"Sayulita Frigate" takes place in Sayulita, a town on the Pacific in Mexico, an hour from Puerto Vallarta, at the south end of the province of Nayarit. At the time of this poem, Sayulita was a still largely undiscovered surf town with dirt streets and sand beaches. Now too-well loved, its charming grit is mostly gone. A frigate is a predatory seabird, common on Mexico's Pacific coast, with a distinctive boomerang shape as it flies overhead.

"Loppers" is a haiku.

"The Ones Who Walk" was written on the death of science fiction novelist Ursula K. Le Guin (1929 – 2018). Her widely anthologized story "The Ones Who Walk from Omelas" pictures a Utopian city where residents have everything they want, if just one child suffers without consolation or end. This poem is a ballad, which is a poem of four-line stanzas with a meter that alternates every other line.

"Lettuce" and "Bananas" are ghazals. In a ghazal, couplets end with the same word at the close of each stanza. As with most modern renditions of this ancient Persian form, to make the intricacies work in English, these two adhere to only some of the traditional Arabic rules.

"Neruda On The Playa" refers to the Chilean poet Pablo Neruda (1904 – 1973), who wrote over two hundred odes on everything from artichokes to socks.

"Signposts and Hedges" is an iambic pentameter sonnet with a Shakespearean rhyme scheme.

"45" makes a reference to Billie Holiday (1915 – 1959), the American jazz and blues singer.

Acknowledgments

Many thanks to the editors of the journals which in order of appearance first published some of these poems:

RHINO:	"Tohubohu"
The Timberline Review:	"On A Deschutes County Road In Winter"
Water~Stone Review:	"Shelter"
	"45"
Pilgrimage:	"Summer In Gorge Country"
	"Sayulita Frigate"
Atlanta Review:	"Nabash"
Buddhist Poetry Review:	"The Hemlock On Top of Cape Meares"
	"On Zen Retreat"
	"The Crack"
The Midwest Quarterly:	"Tasting At Cadenhead's Whisky Shop, Established 1842"
Anti-Heroin Chic:	"What It's About"
Diamond Dust:	"Compassion"
Tipton Poetry Journal:	"Mexican Carnival"
Nostos:	"Yojo"
Heart:	"Gulf"
Fridays On the Boulevard:	"Nirvana"
	"Lettuce"
North Dakota Quarterly:	"Memento Mori"
The Lyric:	"My Inferno"
Amsterdam Quarterly:	"Purgatory"
Kosmos:	"Visiting My Brother's Nebraska Farmstead On August 30th At Dusk"
	"Signposts and Hedges"

"On A Deschutes County Road In Winter" was reprinted in the first and second editions of *Listening To Poetry: An Introduction For Readers and Writers*.

About the Author

David Melville, who grew up in rural Nebraska, began writing poetry in his thirties after moving to Portland, Oregon. His poems have appeared in national and international journals such as *Water~Stone Review, Atlanta Review, Tipton Poetry Journal, Amsterdam Quarterly, The Timberline Review, Pilgrimage,* and *RHINO*. His work has also been anthologized in the college textbook, *Listening to Poetry: An Introduction for Readers and Writers.*

For many years he earned his living as a lawyer. After graduating with highest distinction from the University of Nebraska College of Law where he was an executive editor of the Nebraska Law Review, he argued appeals in Portland. Along the way he taught law as a visiting professor at the University of Illinois, published legal scholarship, practiced commercial litigation at a Portland law firm, represented the poor as a legal-aid lawyer, and clerked for two federal judges. During weekends and sabbaticals, he pursued his passion for literature and history, earning an M.A. in the liberal arts at Reed College, where he wrote a novel as his thesis.

Midway through life's journey, despite the career, he found himself lost in the dark wood Dante wrote of, half-asleep, the path nowhere in sight. He began to immerse himself in different wisdom traditions, Western and Eastern; modern, ancient, and indigenous. Eventually he let go of the law to devote his time to writing and endeavors such as organizing free daily meditations led by spiritual teachers during the pandemic, attended by hundreds around the world. He currently lives in Oregon with his wife Katie, their son Finneas, and their polydactyl cat Luna.

www.ingramcontent.com/pod-product-compliance
Lightning Source LLC
Chambersburg PA
CBHW030058170426
43197CB00010B/1576